How to Take Excellent Care of Senior Citizens

How to Take Excellent Care of Senior Citizens

SPECIAL SECRET RESOURCE!

The Ultimate Eldercare Resource - How To Take Care Of Those Who Took Care Of You

Are You Lethargic When It Comes To Taking Care Of Your Old Parents? Or, Maybe You Care, But You Can't Squeeze In The Time To Spend With Them? Don't Let This Sheer Lack Of Gratitude Set A Bad Example For Your Children, Who Will Probably Do The Same One Day!

Finally! You Can Now Have Instant Access To An All-in-one Guide To Help You Deal With Your Ageing Parents! Learn Some Highly Effective Tips To Make Your Elders Feel Special, Without Stressing Yourself Out Or Sacrificing Your Health...and Truly Feel Good About It From Within!

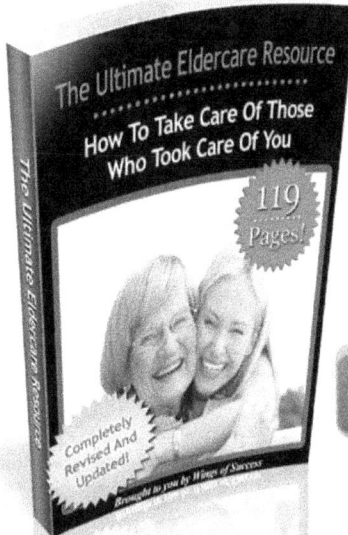

AVAILABLE ONLY FOR A VERY LIMITED TIME!

"**Revealed: How To _Reverse_ The Pain From Sciatica Or A Herniated Disk In Just 48 Hours _Or Less_ Directly From The Comfort Of Your Own Home!!!**"

My *Fail Proof* Back Pain Elimination System, Uncovering A Power-Pack Of Hidden Secrets, Hard-Core Knowledge And Cutting Edge Tools...

Showing You E-X-A-C-T-L-Y Step-By-Step And Detail By Scrawny Little Detail...

How To Eliminate Back Pain Out Of Your Life Totally 110% So It Never Rears Its Ugly Awful Face Ever Again!!!!

Every Video, Audio And PDF Will Show You My Exact Formula For Eliminating Back Pain. For Instance, You Will Discover...

DOWNLOAD NOW

How to Take Excellent Care of Senior Citizens

Contents

- A Caregiver's Guide To Coping With Stress 8
- Caring For The Elderly: Working With Their Money 10
- Coping With Unreasonable Behaviour When Caring For The Elderly 12
- Effective Caring For Your Elderly Relatives: Home Help 14
- Going To A Better Place 16
- Keeping It At Arm's Length 18
- Listening To Your Parents Even Now 20
- Managing Your Senior Citizen's Medications 22
- Quality Of Life For Your Senior Citizen 24
- Taking Care Of Yourself Is Part Of The Job 26
- The Basics Of Caring For The Elderly: Pressure Sores 28
- The Golden Rule Of Caring For The Elderly Revealed! 30
- The Greatest Loss Of Them All 32
- The Layman's Guide To Parkinson's Disease 34
- Watching Your Step: Avoiding And Dealing With Falls Whilst Caring For The Elderly 36
- Adult Day Care Center – A Place For The Elderly 38
- Caring For The Elderly- A Stressful Job 40
- The Basics Of Personal Hygiene For The Elderly 42
- 4 Most Common Ailments Affecting The Elderly 44
- Administering Wound Care And First-Aid To The Elderly 46
- Rebuilding Self Esteem Among The Elderly 48
- Easing Into Care Giving 50
- Outings For The Elderly – A Walk In The Park? 52
- Giving Thanks For Being A Caregiver 54
- Avoiding Guilt Pangs In The Elderly 56
- Safeguarding The Health Of The Elderly 58
- Protecting The Elders From Scams And Rip-Offs 60
- Making A Difference-Involving The Elderly In Social Service 62
- Respecting The Rights Of Senior Citizens 64
- Taking Care Of Yourself As Well As The Elderly: Vacation And Respite 66
- The Best Activities To Stimulate Mentally Ill Seniors 68
- 5 Ways To Maintain Your Health While Caring For The Elderly 70
- The Caregiver's Enemy No.1 72
- The Caregiver's Emotions 74
- Moving Your Elderly Parents Into Your Home – A Boon Or Bane? 76

A Caregiver's Guide To Coping With Stress

Showing care and concern for the elderly fraternity, be it your own family or any stranger, can be extremely pleasing and rewarding. There is a lot of satisfaction involved in this. But this, for some, could also be very upsetting and frustrating. You will hardly know this if you have never been involved in this sort of an issue earlier in your life. It can make you very pessimistic and put you on the downfall track of burnout. It will take a lot from you to recoup yourself and get your acts together. It is no temporary action as you need to be at it full time, even if you are elsewhere. Thus it becomes very important to know to recognize the frustration and stress involved and how to cope with it.

Caregivers also experience a similar case off trauma and stress over a period of time just like a person taking care of an elderly relative. The upsetting part would be the elderly person, after sometime, turn at you and not recognize you for all the work you had done. It is very disturbing for sure even though this could be an extreme example taken into consideration. There are various other sources of stress when it comes to taking care of elders. Non-compliance with requests, threatening, violence or even intolerable behavior, confusion and illness are certain other things which cause the problem. You might have to put in extra effort sometimes on full time basis and this could be tiring. Even if you are not working on full time basis with a particular elder it is extremely hard. Your mind will tend to stagnate on this issue and its tough switching your mind. All your focus might be directed to this and thereby losing control over things.

Recognizing the symptoms before it strikes you is very important. During stress, you will figure out that it is difficult to eat and sleep properly. Lack of sleep and a depressing mood can let you down. You will burst into tears for no good reason and this could be a problem sometimes. The feeling of emptiness has an adverse effect as you will know that you have nothing left and you don't have a choice but to continue. Lethargy will result and frustration starts to creep on you. You might be even directing your irritation to the person you taking care of at that time. You will have very less time to devote for your family and friends as all your time will be taken up here. Hence, your life will totally revolve around the person you are taking care of and your mood swings like a pendulum. Whether you can help it or not, your temperament will be under the scanner. You will have to resort to something else if time arises.

How To Take Great Care of Elders

You must show more concern for yourself and your health when such symptoms arises. It is tough to continue your good job if you can be mentally fit. So you should be ready to solve the problem on your own and cope up with it according to your needs of relaxation. A few of them take a break for a while by going on a holiday or anything that sets their mind off it. You can arrange for another person during that time of your relaxation. You will not worry constantly while doing this and this can help you immensely with your heath. A few people go to a counselor to discuss their problems and open out to them. Sometimes people get help from home and this can be all the more helpful.

There is no way to avoid stress that caregivers encounter during their tenure. But you should give importance and time for yourself. Caregivers are no different and they deserve break as well. Taking care of you is of utmost priority. Devote equal time and space for yourself before things get bigger on you. Detecting stress and abstaining from stress can do wonders to you.

Caring For The Elderly: Working With Their Money

If you have taken the responsibility to take care of an elderly relative or any elderly person, your responsibility wouldn't end with just looking after their health. Your responsibility might even go a touch outdoors as you will have the job of watching them throughout the day including their finances. It sometimes will get big on you as taking care of another person's money won't be easy. It takes a little more from you to make a bold decision if you would want to do this. But in reality, this won't be that tough a thing to manage as your senior relative's wealth would have accumulated to a mammoth amount over the years. People effectively have to budget it out at the end of the day, in general. A few tips are given below to make this process simpler for you.

Before you even start to budget the finances of your elderly relative, you will have to know where they stand in terms of wealth. This needs to be done with some kind of organized chart to work on their accounts on a weekly basis. You will have to make sure you can understand the accounts you are tallying so you don't have to attempt anything professional. Household bills and the debts which are yet to be paid need attention before you start your chart on these accounts. Take twelve months as the period of view and do it methodically. This will certainly help you to cut low your duty.

Sort out all the incomes from various sources, be it pension or other sources. After doing this, take notice of all the previous years' payments as it will help you to make a pay out to the elderly relative. This will also enable you to keep in track of the expendable wealth that will be left for general provisions. Income is the most vital thing to test the ability of your budget. It is your responsibility to detect the various sources of this money and keep the bank credits up to the mark. You might be amidst a financial chaos if you fail to keep in track of this. This will put you under the scanner and can create questions about your future as a caretaker. If you can make the proper research of al the above mentioned things, then there is a possibility for you to continue the budgeting.

Allocating money, if you can vicariously expect rainy days in the coming months, will be more than useful. By doing this, you make sure the elderly relative under your care is safe financially. No one knows what is installed for us in the future, and sometimes you have to be thankful for it. However, if the relative decides to have no specialist or any sort of treatment, you might face a quandary. Hence, it is sometimes better off not allocating money preparing for the month as the seniors might seek medical care and help by selling their homes.

Taking care of your elderly relative itself involves a lot of work so managing their budgets won't be easy. It can be a pain sometimes as you will also want to fulfill their other needs simultaneously. Though it takes a lot of effort in doing this, only your help can fetch them water or probably a roof over their head. The companies react adversely of the bills aren't updated so it is better to do all the budgeting pragmatically right from the first day. This will definitely help to cut-down your workload and can have long-term advantages.

Coping With Unreasonable Behaviour When Caring For The Elderly

All of us have experienced our children throwing a tantrum while out on a shopping or in public. Even if the parent tries to calm the situation down, in most cases it only worsens it. Parents, as a result, feel embarrassed and you can only sympathize with them. A parent's emotion is a mixed bag as they would not only feel sorry about it but also call the child everything from moody to spoil. However, the role of caretaker is no different. This sometimes can be more embarrassing and humiliating than a parent-child drama.

If you get used to your job of taking care of an elderly relative or any elderly person for that matter, the whole issue of tantrums can become a part and parcel of your job. If you aren't accustomed to this sort of a situation, it might be difficult to cope up with. If it happens to be your relative, you have no choice but to cope up with all the tantrums they show up on you. It doesn't matter how difficult it might turn out to be, you will be left with no choices. There are ways to cope up with these predicaments too.

Firstly, it would be nice on your part to research on the source of tantrum rather than telling them how humiliating their behavior is. You have to get a little more relaxed about the whole situation and try to understand it better. What the elderly relative is feeling might not even be close to what your frustration is all about. If you multiply yours by ten, it still wouldn't reach the figure of the amount of frustration the elder is going through. Try to imagine yourself being stuck somewhere in your body and having thoughts recurring at the same point preventing from thinking straight. You will end up reacting in the same way as your relative and thus concluding how tough it is.

But all this can help you cope up with the pressure-cooker kind of a situation only to some extent. The unreasonable behavior of these people will provoke more potent feelings in you when it is directed at you in a different manner. There will be no scope for reasoning if this high voltage situation gets personal. You will have to raise your bar and cope up with it. Take breaks from the individual you are taking care of, just for a few moments might help you greatly. If you wish to ignore the behavior you believe is affecting you, then this might even work out for a long time. It can help you have time to gather your thoughts back.

How To Take Great Care of Elders

In most cases, the unreasonable and intolerable behavior lasts for only sometime. It is fact that, we have got to accept, even elderly people can suffer from mental illness and are liable to go through phases just like children do. You will have to fight your way through whatever the case maybe. Since every person is unique, there is no certain definitive way to solve this problem. Listening to music r probably taking a small walk can calm the situation down. You will see yourself building some resistance to this and all of a sudden you will start to have the tolerance and patience to cope up with the elder.

As time would fly, you will be experienced enough to spot the tantrums from the subject concerned and simply ignore it when it comes to you. All this will not happen overnight but eventually. You have the upper hand then since you would have figured out what works best for you. Think of the elderly relative as a child, if it helps. In fact, it is what they are as treating a child is no rocket science compared to dealing with the adult. If you possess the right temperament the situation can be dealt with ease.

Effective Caring For Your Elderly Relatives: Home Help

Taking care of an elderly relative is a very strenuous process and can be very stressful. The fact that it is your relative adds a little bit of extra responsibility on your shoulders. You have no choice but to ensure effective care and you cannot pull off from your commitment that easily. If it is any elder you can afford to maintain a level of detachment from them. There will be a lot of emotions at stake when you take up this job of taking care of an ill elder or a disabled elder. So it isn't easy to detach yourself from them and hence continuing to care and look after them would be a wise thing to do. This has a lot of options, though, owing to the service popularly called home help. It may be called with a different name but the name itself sums up the whole meaning. It is definitely the most effective help if you are in need of help for the elderly relative. These caretakers are dedicated and very helpful.

Home help is usually a service where qualified and experienced caretaker will come to the elderly person's home to help out with various activities such as bathing, dressing or feeding. This will be done according to the need of the elder. But to many bathing and undressing an elder might be disgusting so it is understandable if they do not want to do it. Again, it all treads back to that air of detachment spoken about earlier. The caretaker and the elderly relative should share a good rapport. So appointing another person to do all this while you could take care of the feeding and other simpler stuffs will be the best way.

The caretakers actually take up this job to make good money. The fact that they are properly schooled and mastered in their trade is true and cannot be taken for granted. They can be honest people who can be trusted anytime. These caretakers have to possess certain qualifications to be able to know the nuances of their job. They are trained to tae the stress and pain involved in the profession. So a few people leave the entire responsibility to the caretaker allowing him the freedom to do what he feels is the best. The caretaker is thus ensured with freedom as well as money to go about his work. No caretaker would want to harm so seeking home help would be the right choice.

Most of the caretakers go the homes of the elderly people at least once in a day. They make sure the elder is out of bed, bathed and fed properly with care. A few often choose home help if they need it. Though, two or even three times in a day is the usual routine which caretakers follow, it entirely depends on what the elder is demanding. There will be caretakers who also would be working on full time basis to earn good money. But again, it totally depends on what you want the caretaker to do everyday. If you do not mind spending extra cash, you might as well go for the caretakers who visit you two or three times a day. It usually gets a little expensive that way but the elder for sure is well treated. You can have an interview to filter the caretakers who have approached you and choose them on convenient basis.

Going To A Better Place

In the life of a senior citizen, there might be some massive events. Lot of them can relate themselves in terms of the incredible change of lifestyle which happened to them and to the situation when the aging parent makes a move out of home and settles in an assisted living facility. The decision to be made is very emotional as the mom and dad belonging to the house will have fond memories of it.

Once you are done with the bold decision of moving your parents to an assisted living apartment, the other thing to consider is about the facilities provided to them. There can be a lot of factors involved in this. So it is better to prepare a checklist of things to do to facilitate them. Do not act fussy or stingy when you are preparing the checklist. You should keep in mind that it is for you parents and it will be a place that you will be visiting more than often. So please make sure that mom and dad enjoy the place they are moving to.

The checklist you have decided to prepare has to be spot-on. They need to have the best possible facilities and it is your duty to provide them the comfort zone. An apartment for the elderly people is very different compared to a usual apartment complex. There will be special and specific facilities in terms of the physical plant and the way they function will make you believe it is the right place for them. The important items that ought to be present in your checklist are:

1. Safety
2. Food services
3. Emergency facilities
4. Ability to respond
5. Look and feel of the society.

One advantage you can take home is that your parents will be amidst many seniors and they will not feel left out. Social events will be held often for the elders to enjoy there time and not feel homesick. Try interviewing a few residents residing there to get a feel about the place and to know the activities taking place within the apartment. You will know if there are other elders who can be friendly with your mom and dad and not create problems with them. If you can get the opportunity to allow your parents to stay over there just to get the feel of it, then it might be very useful.

The other important thing you need to worry about is the proximity of the place. It will make things simpler for you as you will not need to run back and forth dozen times a week. Hence, if the apartment is close-by it will surely help you to have an eye o what is happening there and also would be quite comforting for them if you would make a visit frequently.

Even before making a decision about your parent's move to an entirely different place, you must have discussed with all your friends and relatives about what kind of facilities you expect. You should have made early enquiries on the possible apartments available for your mom and dad so that you don't make hasty decisions when you really want them to move.

It is very vital to take your parents along while looking out for homes for them. This will certainly help their case as they will want to live peacefully and happily in the most comforting place. They might even start interacting with all the residents about the various events in the future. This will certainly be a booster as this would mean they are quite enthusiastic about the move. If they take it as an adventure in life, it will be very pleasing for you to move them. If your mom or dad seem happy about the place and the various activities there, nothing is more satisfying.

Keeping It At Arm's Length

Caregivers face a problem when it comes spending time with their family and friends. They often tend to over-do their work that their family and friends are left in the dumps. They get wrapped up in their work, which certainly demands a lot from them, so much that rest of the world seems to disappear. Caretakers do have relationships and responsibilities that they often tend to forget when stuck up in this job. You can be a good caretaker of your aging parent or any elderly person, but you should also know that life after work has to be given some importance.

It is not only bad for your friends and relatives but also you and the elderly person. Getting too obsessed with work is not a healthy sign as it won't be doing any good to you and the elderly parent. Your family or friends would not want you to be overdoing your work and spend very less time with them. It will be disheartening to them to see this happening to you.

Caretakers suffer from loss of sleep or a nervous breakdown working overtime. They even get eating disorders that can lead to their burnout. The best optimum approach would be to keep your work at arm's length and give equal importance to family and friends.

To have a balanced ratio between work and your family, you have to open out to the elderly person you are working with. It sometimes can be easier with elderly parent than just a mere elder person because the parent will surely be able to understand your plight. You can also talk to them on rational basis explaining to them about your other activities and what you would like to achieve beyond caretaking. The parent can definitely come in terms with you and will se to it that you will not give up your life for just mere caretaking. Often they tend to say things like "I wish he'd be here all the time". This can be misleading sometimes. The parent knows that you are a mature adult and you will need to manage life and job responsibilities in the best possible way.

There is another person to whom you will have to work it out with. It is your boss at work. You can be frank to him and explain all your problems back at home. These days, well trained and hard working individuals dominate the business arena. This could very well go your way as they will know what it takes to be caretaking and working at the same time. Your boss will help you with your work as well as sitting with you to solve other issues than just throwing you out. Nowadays, people have an added responsibility of taking care of parents apart from the work at office.

If you have the best understanding with your boss at work, it will do you a world of good. He will be there alongside with you when you will have to take your parent to the hospital or to the doctors. In case of emergency, he will be flexible and allow you to work on other days to make up for it. In fact, many employers allow you to work at home thus giving you ample time to take care of your parents and for other activities as well. A few companies offer extended break programs were you can take a good time off your work to manage your caretaking responsibilities. That is invaluable when you are moving your parent from home to an assisted living environment or when your parent is under the weather.

Solicit the support of your loved ones above all. If your mom has to be at grandmas house every evening for few hours, call up your dad or brother to do some cheese and macaroni so that when she is back her work will be cut-off. You can catch up some food joint nearby if you do not have anyone to make food for you. If your family, your friends and your colleagues can help you out managing both your caretaking as well as work at office, it will be mighty helpful for you. But make sure you see them often and spend quality time with them to ensure their support.

Listening To Your Parents Even Now

Would you ever feel aggravated after knowing that the elder is trying to stop your progress when you go to visit them in their apartment? It feels miserable especially when you do it out of care and concern for them? The list you had prepared earlier no doubt had all the ingredients of a perfect caretaker. It was prepared to help your parents live in a clean and healthier atmosphere.

Being a caregiver is no simple job and for the major part of it you do things that your aging parent isn't able to do any more. A few elders don't have the energy to do so fatigue and other factors such as motivation prevent them from doing anything. Oblige when your parent wants to sit down and talk to you, for all you know it might be very important. It could be aggravating to you, but the news you share with her could be mighty important than the apartment getting cleaned up.

It feels better to be called a caregiver or a care taker than just a maid or a cook or even a chauffeur. A caregiver's job is not easy when compared to the latter as anybody could do such things. Caregivers feel better because the parent you look after is more close to the heart than just any elder. Anything she speaks can be understood better only when you can lend your ears and patiently listen.

You as a companion to your parent will make them extremely proud and happy so do not downplay the role. You will provide a lot of support and emotions to your parent by doing this. This will boot their self esteem. It will encourage them to share anecdotes and their stories with you when you go there to visit them.

A listener is not the one who keeps saying words like "uh huh" often. You have to do better than that to make them feel good. Your parent will feel bad if she finds that you are trying to tolerate her talk and that you aren't really interested. To capture their hearts and make them feel on top of the world is to visit their apartment more often just to hear them share their stories.

You should perhaps make it a routine to visit your parent's apartment to sit down and have a snack or some tea. You can spend a valuable half hour with them. It will be nice on your part to listen to them with lot of interest and thereby cheering them up. You can laugh at their jokes and encourage them to speak more with you. Ask them questions and discuss things in depth to just spur them on to talk more.

You choose an apt time to say things like, "Mom, I shall go tidy up the dishes. You can sit and continue to talk while I am doing it". This will be most encouraging to them. This is a nice way to do both your work as well as listen to your parent. You can let your mom or dad walk around the place following you to tell their stories. Give reactions of you being engrossed in their stories to keep them going.

Do not filter any topics to talk about. Talk in general and be frank to them and most importantly listen with ears wide open to react well. You should be well prepared to even talk trivial issues just like you do with kids. Elders are like children after all. Improve your communication skills with them as you go about talking to them and also make them feel important. They will start to open up when they figure out you are listening to them well.

Managing Your Senior Citizen's Medications

"Old people will need a lot of pills."

One day, the grandson of the granddad observed that his granddad needed a lot of pills. The observation might have been crude, but certainly is a right observation. In reality, we find the senior citizens take a lot of medication and pills everyday. The medications will be so varied that it could be difficult to keep track of it. That is exactly why the aging people possess a dispenser kit where they keep their medicines for a whole week in a systematic order.

More than the type of medication concerned, medicine interaction with the body is important. If you see your parent taking five or six pills or even more pills at a time, the interaction of these medicines with the body might conflict with one another. Medicine if taken in a higher scale becomes an overdose and senior citizens more often find themselves in such a case. They will be prescribed with many medicines from various places and at the end it might not have an effect in the treatment. Consuming alcohol or the country drugs can cause explosive effects on the body.

It is your responsibility as a caregiver to ensure that your parent, be it mom or dad, does not consume country drugs or alcohol. Any drug related reaction can lead to hospitalization and sometimes could be even fatal.

When it comes to managing a parent's medications, knowledge is bliss. Being ignorant about all the medications can cause deep trouble. The pharmacist or the doctor is your key people in case you have any doubts over the medicines your parent is consuming. If you end up getting different prescriptions from different doctors, the body might not respond to the medicines. Each medicine conflicts in the body leading to no cure. So make sure only one doctor is in charge of your parent's health. Interact with your doctor to know why the medicines are actually taken and whether it would have any adverse effect on your parent.

A pharmacist can provide the same help as your doctor. Pharmacist is the one who is trained to understand the work of these drugs. Similarly, it is better to choose one pharmacist and stick with him. You can enquire all about the drugs your parents are consuming and also ask him for timely advices. A pharmacist will know what the drugs exactly do to a person's body and how the body might react to it.

Be it the doctor or pharmacist causing problems for your parent, the next important thing is to make sure your parents have the right medicine at he right time at home. Taking medicines at the wrong time can cause potential problems which can damage the body of the elder. Mark the bottles accordingly so that there is no confusion while having the medicines. Keep it simple for your parents if they have to have the medicines on their own.

Prepare a good and legible timetable for your parent. Buy multicolored bottles in order to store the medicine. Name the bottles cleanly and neatly. The timetable should be prepared in such a way that the parent can easily identify the bottle and consume the medicine. For example, you can have the schedule saying "4 p.m. take 3 from black bottle, 2 from yellow bottle and 1 from red bottle." This can help them a lot and prevent confusion. Make it so clear that there will be no room for misunderstanding.

Keeping track of the expiry dates of the medicines is very vital. Use online reorder services and pharmacies to save a lot of money. They can provide you with generic equivalent of the prescription drugs. Also it is important that you buy the medicines from the right dealer.

By supervising your parent on these medications, you are literally the brain of the whole operation. Your parent, be it mom or dad, may not have that good an eyesight or can be mentally fatigued so you have to absolutely be on top of them to take care of them. Make sure you are always there next to them providing them the necessary medicines at the right time.

Quality Of Life For Your Senior Citizen

It is important to remember that your parents were your caregivers when you were young. They were the ones who ensure that you were safe, clothed, well fed and had the best medical care. They always obliged to spend money on you if it was needed. Being a caregiver, there is more than just providing food and shelter.

It is now you're turn to turn on the tables and take care of your parents. Your parents now need you as a caregiver who can provide them with the basics in life. As they move into their older years, they are now struggling to attend the basic needs of life. You have to be the one who can provide all that to your parents by giving them the right food and keeping them safe. Small things like keeping heir clothes clean and taking responsibility of their medication will do a lot of good to you. You also can manage their finances and ensure they aren't cheated. By managing their finances, you can keep their work cut-off and help them a great deal.

Whether you can, as a caregiver, provide the factor known as "the quality of life" is a question. Your parents gave a lot to you making your childhood nostalgic and really memorable. You had your times of joy, happiness, fun and laughter being part of a lovely family. It is because your parents went beyond a measure to make your life happy and peaceful.

In fact, you can still rejoice all your nostalgic memories of childhood with your parents even now. It was your parents who made your life fabulous and are responsible for all the fun in your childhood. They made sure your life was good and was rich all the way through. Those two people are the ones who now need your help. The people, who have made you what you are now, need assistance and care which you can provide as a caregiver.

So how do you enhance the life of your parents after their retirement years? If you are capable of giving them the joy and happiness, which once you got, it can be very pleasing. It can be a sweet pay back for all they did for so many years. Here are some of the things you can possibly do to keep your parents lively and joyous…

How To Take Great Care of Elders

- **Take them for dinner every week.** If you know when your parents reach home everyday, take them for a surprise dinner. This could be very pleasing and enjoyable to them. Your parents are sure to enjoy this and it will turn out to be a memorable day.
- **Provide them ample family time.** If you happen to live in the same town as your parents, it is expected of you to spend quality time with your parents to keep them rejuvenated. They will cherish every moment of it. Take them to churches or any school activity and make them feel comfortable. During holidays, make them do fun activities and keep them occupied.
- **Make the springs and the summers a festive time for them.** Surprise them often and if you could make your grandpa a Santa Clause it could be fun.
- **Make their house a home.** Being a caretaker, you will sometimes have to take up the responsibility of cleaning up the apartment for them. Do not stop with just cleaning. Stick nice and funny notes to keep them interested. Also stick their favorite cut-outs on the walls and shelves. Make them feel comfortable just like home and try to provide that air of freshness to that place.

If you can do all this to your parents, just like they provided you the fun, joy and the sense of "home", you can feel that you have given them a little back of what had been given to you in your childhood.

By repaying the love and the fun times to your elderly parents, there is a real value attached to it. These can rejuvenate your parent and can keep their health at bay. It is therapeutic and can help them relive their old times. Put on more effort to keep them very happy and more importantly occupied and see them blossom in life.

Taking Care Of Yourself Is Part Of The Job

Being a primary caregiver is tough and it is universally known that the job of becoming one is a difficult transition in life. It is extremely tough to go through a reversal of parent and child in a family. It was your mom and dad who where the strong ones earlier telling you things like, "It is ok, everything will be fine soon". They encouraged you and helped you out when it was most needed.

But as your parent starts aging, things start to change a bit. This is especially when your parent is going through a tough period health wise and is going to kick the bucket soon. When you know that your parents are soon approaching death, it becomes highly difficult to cope up with your daily challenges as well as your life in general. It will take a lot from you to stay upbeat and active.

Caring for an elderly person can be immensely satisfying and overwhelming. You will have to face their financial, medical and other problems though. If they are battling a disease or soon approaching death, you have to have concerns over their health and mental state. The parent will love to be cared but you will have to do a lot of work to block them mentally and emotionally sometimes.

You tend to feel very disturbed and distressed when your parent is on the death bed. It is very disheartening to watch your parent deteriorate. A caregiver, hence, must give his 100% to his parent who is soon to approach a certain outcome.

The general problem with caregivers is that they have other obligations too apart from taking care of their loved ones. You will need to spend enough quality time with your family and also keep your health good. So it is very important for caregivers, the family of caregivers and even the one being cared for to open their eyes and be aware of a caregiver burnout. It is equally important for the caregiver to take care of himself if he so badly wants to take care of his loved ones.

A caregiver sometimes develops guilt which isn't very healthy. It can keep building and the outcome is not very fruitful. They feel guilty for not only their mom or dad's sickness but also for the fact that they have other issues in life. They know they can't devote time for his family needs and thus feel guilty about it. Guilt is a powerful force that can let a person down easily.

A burnout to a caregiver can result in the decline in health of the caregiver and also what it does is change the attitude and approach of the caregiver. A nervous breakdown can be very serious when it strikes a caregiver. Lack of sleep and loss of appetite are the first signs of this burnout. When this happens, it bogs down the caretaker massively. H should ensure he is in perfect health in order to help his parent. As a result of all this, the caregiver will be unable to understand the needs of his parent.

If you can spot these symptoms of a burnout in yourself or any person, act swift to get some medication. Taking care of oneself is a major part of the whole caretaking process.
There can even be situations were the elderly person it self spots the fatigue in the caretaker and sends him back home giving him a break. This will do a lot of good to this caretaker as taking care of oneself is as important as taking care of the parent. If there is a good understanding between the caretaker and the elderly person, the caretaker can afford to spend time for himself and is family.

The Basics Of Caring For The Elderly: Pressure Sores

As a caretaker, it is very important to know the elder person's wants and needs. You will have to provide them either mentally or by conversing with them. You might have to look after them keenly in order to keep them satisfied and happy. Pressure sores can start off like a simple cut in a hand but can soon become a gaping wound when it is not treated immediately. The wound will be very severe as it can travel right till the tissues and bones and it will be tough to recoup from it. Caretakers have to be on their toes while taking care of the elder in order to prevent these pressure sores to get bigger on them. This is a quick guide to help you out from pressure sores. It is better to treat them early as it can have massive effect on caretakers.

Pressure sores are developed as a result of sedentary activities. In other words, it is a tissue which starts to deteriorate when a person tends to sit or lie down for long periods of time. That piece of skin will be overworked and hence causes the crack and tear. Blood flow to that particular part of the skin will be restricted and if one does not restore the blood supply to that region, the sore will develop into a huge one. It is a mere red mark in the area but this has tendencies to get bigger if left unnoticed. A pressure sore doesn't usually disappear immediately and this should alert you that the area needs inspection. Detecting them at early stages of its formation can help you suffer less.

These pressure sores might begin to form in body parts such as the lower back, legs, bottom and the ankles. Basically, it occurs in all places where blood flow is possible and especially in places where there is not great amount of fat. By rolling, turning and adjusting techniques you can prevent pressure sores from occurring. If they are present already, it might help in healing them. Turning will certainly help in restoring the blood supply in that are and thus trying to heal it. Nursing homes generally employ this trick. It is better to move the elder, though comfortable, to prevent sores than to let it grow and get bigger. You will have to make them understand that pressure sores are painful.

Antiseptic cushioning pads containing antiseptic cream to kill germs can help to treat these sores. The area affected should be kept clean else it gets infected more. If at all it gets infected, it will clearly be seen. The pressure sore gets deeper and deeper if left without medication and it can be dangerous when it creates a hole in the skin. It has an obnoxious smell of rotting flesh in addition to some pus formation. Betadine solution or salt water can be used to treat these sores. Dressings have to be changed frequently and in order to aid healthy healing and prevent germs dead cells within the pressure sore have to be removed.

Pressure sores can create huge problems for the caretaker. But if it is nipped in the bud at early stages, it can be prevented from doing further damage. Care should be taken to avoid the redness in the skin as it is the first sign of a pressure sore. Once you experience the pain of these pressure sores, you will go any distance to prevent it from occurring the next time. Studying about the pressure sores can be very helpful when it comes to treatment. If the elder is moved regularly then there is no need for you to worry about any pressure sore.

The Golden Rule Of Caring For The Elderly Revealed!

Being a caretaker, irrespective of whether you are the care assistant visiting an apartment or being a caretaker of your parent at home, is no simple job. It might be difficult to know where to start and what to do. Caretaking is definitely a demanding job with daunting tasks ahead of you all the time. You will have to know the basics just like when you attempt to ride a bicycle. There is no course or guide to tell you what to do or how to react in different situations. Each caregiver can be unique and can have his own technique when it comes to the trade. But however, there exists a golden rule for all the caregivers. It says- always have a routine and never ever underestimate its power!

Routines find it very important when a caretaker is trying to have good vibes with the elderly person he is working with. With routines, he can make the elder feel extremely happy and give them an air of support and comfort. Enquiring about the senior is the first and most significant step before framing the routine. If the elder taken care of is your parent, this shouldn't really be a problem for you. But routines are a must even if it is any stranger to you. It is almost impossible to start a routine without knowing anything about the person under your assistance. A good routine can be developed for the elderly person if there is a good rapport and compromise between the caretaker and the elder.

Always it is better to build and cement your place in the heart of the elder. Compromising and respecting each other can help you to know the person a lot better. Preparing a routine before this can cause problems. However logical and effective the routine may be, unless you the person head to toe, you might end up in a predicament. Build the trust and respect with your elder before he sabotages or mucks up your routine badly.

A proper and well prepared routine can have long term benefits to the elderly person. It can make his life very happy and peaceful if the routine you prepare is worthy. The routine acts as an alarm to let you know what to do at different times and thereby helping the senior citizen to have less stressful time. What a routine can do is make the elder feel very comfortable as nothing is going to be unexpectedly thrown at him.

How To Take Great Care of Elders

A routine can help you to keep track of what you doing and how the medications are going. Unnecessary frustration and annoyance can be avoided if you have a well prepared routine. It can give the elders some kind of control over their lives. It might take a long time to prepare the routine for an elder, but once it is done you will hardly want to deviate from that. Routines can guide you properly and the chances of going wrong at any point are very less.

You will realize how effective this tool called as routine can be. It gives you a control of what is happening and prevent any sort of confusion. It cuts down unwanted stress. Though it is not easy doing a routine, it has immense rewards when use to its maximum. Routines help to stay cool and comfortable throughout the process. It will be worth all the efforts put in by you and the elder will appreciate your effort. Don't make it too late as these routines, as we saw, have massive advantages. You will never know until you complete the whole routine how useful it can be. It can either be used as an introductory step or the last resort in the caretaking process.

The Greatest Loss Of Them All

The hardest thing you can face as a caretaker or even as a normal person is the loss of one of your parents. It is a traumatic time for you as well as your family and it takes a lot in you to cope up with his demise. More than he being your mom's husband and grandpa of several grandchildren, you having lost your daddy feels terrible. So how do you help your mom to get through these tough times?

There will be a time where you will need the support and understanding of your spouse and kids too. You have to stay brave for your children considering you and your widowed mom is feeling extremely difficult. You have got to support them hands down to help them through their way to forget what had happened.

The whole purpose of the funeral is that even the ones who are not close to the family feel closure that this wonderful life has gone on to his reward. There could be a sense of relief in you and your family if your dad had died after being ill for a long time. If the doctor had given no hopes for his survival, you would have had enough time to realize that he needn't suffer any longer and that death could well be the better thing for him.

You will have to be there for your mother who had just been widowed. She will need you alongside for a shoulder to cry as well as some mental support. Grief surfaces in very strange ways. Sometimes it can strike you at the funeral or sometimes it hits you ten days after the death of the elder.

Usually after the group processing of the loved elder, when the family gets home and routine work starts, you are expected to say with your mom to help her feel comfortable. This is mostly when grief surfaces. The transition might take place slowly but it is very essential for you to stay with her and help her out.

Grief tends to be selfish when it occurs. We can put up a sad face and tell people that the death has greatly affected us but in reality, it is the spouse who feels miserable after living for so many years with the person. She can feel lost and lonely after the death of your dad and so you have got to be there to lend her the supporting hand. Dinner time and other potential time can be used to talk through to make her feel that the one departed had to really go and that no one could have prevented that from happening.

As a caregiver, make sure you visit home more often without having dry spells. It can do a world of good to her as she will find herself very comfortable when you are around. Eventually she might learn to cope up with the loss alone, but it is better to be with her till the transition state.

There will surely be a time when she will cry her heart out to let her grief leave her. It is the most important period of time which you will have to spend with her. Do not try to come up with any comforting lines. Being present there can be very comforting by itself. Helping her around with the dishes and giving her a sip of wine can prove to be very consoling.

Finally and most importantly, talk about the departed elder often to your mom. She might feel happy about the fact that he is still remembered. Discuss his good deeds and anything about him to make her feel he is still around. Take a beak from your daily activities to sit down and talk about all he is done in his life and how good a man he was. You can even narrate a few stories which he had been involved in to keep her occupied. Talk about the things he has done as a father to you and how he had been a wonderful father all your life.

The joy and happiness of these times when revered can be really healing for the elderly person as well as for you. Just when you do all this, you will start to do some serious groundwork for an important caretaking responsibility in your hand for the future.

The Layman's Guide To Parkinson's Disease

As an adult, you have to prepare yourself for any calamity coming your way. A few thins will be inevitable when you get old. But in spite of your awareness and preparation, there are a few diseases which cannot be stopped from attacking you. Parkinson's disease is one such disease which you cannot prepare for. It mainly attacks elder persons though younger people are also liable to be attacked by it. Medically, it is related to the brain but most of them believe it occurs because of mental degeneration. It can be extremely stressful to watch a person suffering from his type of disease as it progressively deteriorates the condition. The elder will only know the starting point of this disease as it all happens in a hurry after that.

Nerve cells in a body cause Parkinson's disease. They slowly break down and thus preventing any signal conveyance to the brain. The nerve cells connect the body and the brain and let the brain know what the body is doing or vice versa. This disease can prevent this from happening as the nerve cells get damaged slowly. Sufferer starts to lose control over things and it becomes extremely difficult to manage his body.

Symptoms are plenty for this kind of a disease. Earliest of the symptoms could be the shaking of arms, hands, legs and jaw of a person. Nerves which are deteriorating affect the muscles and its movement. These symptoms can get worse as time goes by and it becomes noticeable to people around you. The disease affects one part of the body more than the other and it affects al sorts of communications. The tremors not only cause the nerves to weaken more, but also affect the speech of the person. The big shakes of hands and legs usually start after a year of tremors continuously for a few. Sometimes, for a few sufferers it takes hardly any time before these tremors strike them.

Doctors, as of yet, do not know how this Parkinson's disease is caused despite the extensive and extravagant researches being done. Right now, there is no real test to diagnose this disease in a patient. The diagnosis done is based on medical histories and the tests taken to rule out other illnesses and ailments. This basically means there is no cure for this disease. So once if you have acquired this disease, it is going to be there for life. Many try to get used to it and resume their daily activities, but there will be a point when it can get terrible and intolerable.

It mainly causes depression in people as they find it difficult to go about their daily work. Dressing and unbuttoning could be like the impossible mazes to conquer.

One can alleviate the symptoms of Parkinson's disease using certain drugs. This is only for a short term though. A few medications have the effect of stopping the tremors for some period of time and thus helping the sufferers to go on with their normal life. There are certain drugs available in the market. Carbidopa-levodopa, Selegiline, Bromocriptine, Ropinirole, Pergolide and Tolcapone are a few drugs which helps the above case. Though they have different brand names, they are slated to do the same work. These drugs don't suit everyone. A few tend to get better with these while a few suffer more at the hands of these drugs. No body knows which work better so even the doctors take chances.

Parkinson's disease is something no one should get as it can disturb not only the sufferer but also the people around. There is very little that could be done to save people from this terrible disease. If diagnosed early, it can prove to be effective though it can sometimes go out of hand. Research is still going on to find a cure. Till then you and I have no choice but to get on with life.

Watching Your Step: Avoiding And Dealing With Falls Whilst Caring For The Elderly

Caretakers should take advices from anyone who has had a decent stint as a caretaker in the past. Their experience can prove to be very handy as they can tell you about the hazards and pitfalls involved in this profession. One advice you are sure to hear from these people is the danger of falls at anytime. The elder community has an appalling number of falls every year. This is mainly because they are quite weak and unstable on their feet. Their bodies are not conducive for stable postures and thus liable to any fall anytime. Repeated falling causes harm and this can happen if their bodies aren't very agile. Bones become brittle can be broken easily as they are old. Elders are known for dislocating their hips or even fracturing them on a fall. The pain it causes is excruciating and can stay like that for a long time. You need to be aware of these and try to prevent it from happening.

Prevention is better than cure and certainly so with these elders. Preventing such mishaps can be vital for both you, as a caretaker, as well as the senior. Monitoring the senior citizen and maintaining the safety of the elderly person I such a difficult thing to do even if you have eyes at the back of your head. It takes a while to get used to their movements, routines and habits. Watching them at close quarters can help you to anticipate their movement and thereby preventing their fall. If you can spot any danger from a distance, it can help you from preventing any disastrous fall of the senior. But as a primary caretaker, you have to get used to it though this cannot be a long term solution.

The primary step you must do to prevent falls and trips of elderly people has nothing to do with the subject concerned itself. You should be focusing on the immediate environment rather. Try to eliminate all the possible falling hazards at home. Remove rugs or carpets which are loose and used for decorating rooms. All these sort of small problems can cause big problems in the future. Zimmer frames can be attached to these beds to prevent falls especially in the night. These are specially made for people with unsteady feet.

If the fall of an elderly citizen has already taken place, you should have the head to deal with the issue than chickening out. You should be clear about what you are going to do rather than feeling perturbed by the situation. First thing you should be doing is remove all the obstructions that caused the fall of the elder. Assess the place and time of fall. First aid is mandatory and so it should be immediately into effect. Do not try moving the person as long as you know the elder is perfectly alright without any bones or limbs damaged. In case of a head injury, call the ambulance quickly as head injuries could be fatal sometimes. Keep the relatives warm about the whole situation and ask them not to panic.

Falls are quite unpredictable at home and you should always have the temperament to deal with it. With no doubt, you will have to experience that at some point in life, no matter how well prepared you are. Taking precautionary measures can reduce the number of falls and also reduce the severity of the injuries sustained by the elder.

Adult Day Care Center – A Place For The Elderly

Our elderly parents very often need our support to help them to settle in their retired lives. While trying to find a solution to the issue, we may come across all types of services that are available for taking care of senior citizens. Due to your preoccupation with a job and having your own family to look after, you may not be able to provide them support. In such a case, adult day care can prove to be a blessing for many. Adult day care is beneficial to those senior citizens who need the company of people during daytime.

However, when you decide to utilize the services of an adult day care center for your elderly mother or father, ensure that they are also involved in the decision – making. The thought of adult day care center is very upsetting for an elderly parent, because it gives them a feeling of being neglected, or being treated as an infant who needs looking after. It is best to avoid using the phrase 'adult day care' while making the suggestion, as the elderly are sensitive people and may think you are putting them away, someplace.

There may be church programs in your local parish that the senior citizens can attend to pass their time rewardingly, and many prefer to do so. The other option is, of course, a day care center where they can enjoy the company of other like minded people. The ideal way to find a suitable adult day care center is to conduct a tour along with your elderly parent to find out what options exist locally, and make the choice together. You may, however want to get some prior information regarding the adult day care center by making enquiries with them. Some of the pertinent questions could be:

- Is transportation facility available at the assisted care facilities? Does that facility continue to operate all day? This is needed so that your parent does not get stranded at the facility for lack of transportation.
- Do they have qualified medical personnel to attend to the elderly, in case there is any kind of medical emergency?
- Is there an arrangement for food and beverages for a day-long stay? Are the food services sensitive to diet restrictions prescribed by the doctor? This would be a pertinent question if your parent is a diabetic and has to follow a restricted diet.

How To Take Great Care of Elders

- How many elders are present at the care center on any given day? Too few would imply that the center is not providing good service and too many would mean lack of attention for your parent in the large crowd.
- What are the costs involved?

The activities and entertainment provided for the elderly at the adult day care center are an incentive for them to go there. For example, during the football season, if the center provides a place for all the men to gather and cheer for the game, it will be more enjoyable for your dad rather than being alone in the apartment watching the game. If the adult day care center has a variety of activities like card games or puzzles that appeal to everyone, then it will be a fun place for your parent to pass their time.

Arranging for a good adult day care center to take care of your elderly father or mother takes a load off your mind. Before making a decision to select the center for your parent, it would be a good idea to get a feel of the place by talking to the staff and spending some time yourself to gauge the atmosphere. This way, you are sure that your parent is well taken care of and passing the time in a healthy and friendly environment. They will get to know more people and generally enjoy the time spent at the center. This will prove to be invigorating for them and they will eat and sleep better, thus solving a number of problems associated with old age.

Caring For The Elderly- A Stressful Job

Taking care of an elderly person is stressful to say the least. By the time you accept the fact that you are required to take care of the aging parent, your help is urgently needed. You have some catching up to do in the role of a primary caregiver to your elderly parent, in the form of controlling their finances and lifestyle and taking stock of their medical situation.

Very often, neither the caregiver nor the person being cared for has volunteered for the job. The caregiver may not like to be burdened with the additional responsibility. The senior citizen may be hostile, resistant or downright disagreeable causing much stress to both the individuals involved. Since these may be your parents you are taking care of, you are used to obeying their instructions. But since the roles have now been reversed, the fact is difficult to accept for both, the parent and the child.

You may have certain expectations from your siblings or your own high standards. When these expectations are not met, it leads to frustration. As a caregiver, one has to learn to compromise. Your parents may need constant attention which you may not be in a position to provide. Realistically speaking, spending as much time as possible with your aged parents after taking care of your family, your job, housework and yourself, would be a reasonable expectation.

The individual entrusted with the role of primary caregiver must recognize that the stress levels in his life will increase. Stress is deemed to be one of the major causes of mental or physical health problems in adults. When stress levels begin to overwhelm you and become difficult to cope, you may end up with health problems of your own. This is not the best of situations, as this will affect you as well as the person being cared for and even the rest of the family.

It is a struggle for one person to manage the job of looking after the aged parents. The family of the caregiver should be supportive and involve themselves in the activity as much as possible, to share the burden. If you are not living close to your aged parents, and your sibling is looking after them, make efforts to help out as much as possible by calling up the parents regularly or helping in any other way you can. Avoid nagging suggestions to the caregiver, even though they may be meant for the good of the parents. Make sure to communicate your gratefulness and support to your sibling so that he or she is not made to feel alone in this endeavor.

As an individual, you can deal with the stress levels yourself. Your aged parents depend on you, being the primary caregiver. So it is as much your duty to take care of yourself for their sake. This way you can be a better caregiver, lead a stress free life and take care of all your responsibilities as well. This should be the healthy approach to elderly care, if it is to be long term responsibility that you will need to fulfill.

The Basics Of Personal Hygiene For The Elderly

Personal hygiene is an important aspect of an individual's routine. Every individual takes care to remain fresh through the day. You wake up each morning, brush your teeth, shower and deodorize yourself. A break in this routine will give you a feeling of being dirty and cause depression and frustration. Unfortunately, personal hygiene may become an issue for the elderly, due to illness or bad health. When elderly people are unable to take care of this routine of personal hygiene, they need assistance from another individual. It is necessary to set up a daily routine for the personal hygiene of any elderly person you are entrusted with.

It is essential to build up trust with the person that you are responsible for caring. You can talk them through the routine you will be setting up for their daily care and hygiene, the first few times. This will help them to know what to expect and may help them relax a bit. Most elders are reluctant to let someone else administer their personal hygiene. It gives them a sense of being dependent and having lost their dignity. This may cause them to react angrily or verbally abuse the caregiver. This is understandable under the circumstances, and one can try to see their point of view to appreciate what they are going through. Therefore, a lot of patience and understanding is required to administer personal hygiene to the elderly.

If the senior can take care of at least a small part of their personal hygiene, they must be encouraged to do so. This will give them a feeling of achievement and independence and also help to lift up their spirits. Even a small thing done by them is better than nothing at all. The routine established for a senior's personal hygiene should include washing, deodorizing and brushing teeth. These are integral parts of personal hygiene and should be undertaken daily. Other small activities can be added to the routine depending upon the individual's need. For instance, in case of women, if they like to put on make up, then this should also be encouraged.

Maintaining the personal hygiene for the elderly will promote physical well being and mental health. You may be able to detect any bodily changes that may take place in the form of lumps or bruises, if you perform the washing routine for the senior. By noting the changes in the body, you are creating a kind of record that can alert you to any potential illnesses. This will help in early diagnosis of any potential health problems that may arise in future.

Personal hygiene is a sensitive area and most elders are reluctant to entrust this work to another person. Personal hygiene for the elderly must be handled with tender care and patience. It helps to build up trust and creates a bond between both the persons involved in the activity.

4 Most Common Ailments Affecting The Elderly

As an individual grows older, he becomes more susceptible to various ailments and illnesses that may render him incapacitated in some way or other. This is a sad fact of life and every one of us has to face this eventuality at some point. However, not all ailments affecting the aged are incurable, only a few are untreatable. There are many ailments affecting the elderly that a caregiver comes across and learns to cope with. It is painful to watch a loved one succumb to a disease, but this is an inevitable fact. Some background information on a few ailments may help preparation for the worst.

1. **Cancer**: This is the most serious of all ailments. Over two thirds of the elderly are affected by this disease. Lung and breast cancer are the most common, with skin cancer making the occasional appearance. Cancer can be treated successfully nowadays, but the success rate is low in aged patients. Senior citizens are not strong enough to cope with the course of chemotherapy. An early diagnosis of cancer increases the chances of a full recovery. Thus, any anomaly should be checked out immediately by a medical professional.

2. **Dementia**: A large number of seniors suffer from Dementia. Dementia is caused due to damage of the connections between the brain and nerve endings. This ailment is not curable and its causes are unknown. There is no effective treatment for this disease, but some drugs may help to temporarily control the symptoms. The most potent and common form of Dementia is Alzheimer's Disease. The symptoms of Alzheimer's disease build up gradually over a period of a few years. It is frustrating for the patients as they become more and more confused and lose all their memory.

3. **Parkinson's disease**: This is another disease related to the nerve cells, and its causes are yet unknown. Dementia affects the mental health of the individual whereas Parkinson's disease is primarily a physical disability. The symptoms of Parkinson's are uncontrollable shaking of the limbs, that is just as frustrating. There is no cure for this disease, although it may be contained to some extent for a short period, with the use of drugs. After a certain period, the symptoms cannot be controlled.

4.   Diabetes: This ailment is a result of bad diet and considered to be a lifestyle disease. High fat and sugar intake may be the causative factors. Diabetes is caused due to the body's inability to produce insulin to keep blood sugar levels under control. This disease is curable with diet and medication either in injection or tablet form. Great attention must be paid to wounds in diabetics as the wounds have a tendency to degenerate faster than a non-diabetic. The result may be amputation of limbs, which is quite common. Hence, a swift diagnosis and treatment is necessary for Diabetes.

Administering Wound Care And First-Aid To The Elderly

It is extremely hard work to maintain the health of an elderly member of the family. Often it is an uphill task and one feels frustrated with the lack of response in terms of the health of the aged member. Even with sheer hard work and dedication, if you manage to turn around the situation, there is always some setback with rise of a new health problem. Most of the elders due to their delicate physical conditions and especially those with mental or physical disabilities are susceptible to minor injuries. It is therefore, very essential for a caregiver to have basic knowledge of treatment for wounds and small injuries to deal with such situations.

The most common injuries are minor cuts and scrapes which may be the results of small accidents. These cuts and bruises may look harmless and at times, the elders may not even realize their existence. Such minor injuries may become quite serious in case of the elderly, if they are not treated in time. All such minor injuries should be cleaned, disinfected and dressed immediately upon happening. These wound should not be left unattended as infection may set in. It may sound ridiculous; after all, it is only a minor cut or scrape we are talking about. However neglecting to treat the wounds, may cause serious problems later on because, the infection takes place faster in case of older people. Therefore, a caregiver must be extra vigilant and provide first aid to the elders as soon as possible.

The caregiver must attend a basic first aid course in the initial stages. The community colleges offer basic first aid courses that cover the relevant aspects of wound care for the elderly. Some of the course content is usually common sense, but it helps to be imparted practical training by an instructor, so that you can remember it when the need arises. Even if you have taken a first aid course earlier, it is advisable to take a refresher course that is more specific to elder care. These courses will also include training in wound care.

Another important aspect of wound care is ensuring that the individual has been given the preventive shots on schedule. The Tetanus shot is especially important, as tetanus is the most serious infection that can be contracted. A small open wound will help the infection to spread via the bloodstream. Thus, the most important aspect of wound care is prevention of infection.

Wound care is simple enough to learn for any caregiver, and it can be easily managed with a little practice. It is important to be aware of this aspect of elder care, because neglecting it will create problems which may become unmanageable in the future. Timely care of small injuries in the elderly will ensure great dividends in terms of their general well being and health.

Rebuilding Self Esteem Among The Elderly

Self esteem is an integral part of an individual's mental makeup and human psychology. It is an image we have about ourselves, how we feel, how we react to our work, our relationships with family and in general, how we socialize in the community as a whole. Self esteem is viewed as the basis of human psychology and each person is quite aware of their own self esteem. The same awareness of self esteem is present in the elderly, though it may change with the changes in the lifestyle and a change in the roles. As the elderly people become more and more dependent on others, they begin to feel they are unimportant, and that others also perceive them to be so.

Caring for the elderly may not be your first experience at care giving. You may have been performing the role of a caregiver to your children by taking care of their psychological and emotional needs. Self esteem is an important aspect of child psychology too and it is crucial to their success later in life. As the caregiver for your elderly parent, you may have to perform the same functions, though you are not 'raising them'. That means you have to take care of their physical health, their finances, their living arrangements and their self esteem and mental health as well.

As an individual, one cannot empathize with the elderly parents due to the constant changes that go on in their lives and the great impact it has on their self esteem. Your own sense of self esteem stems from the fact that you are an independent individual and your ability to provide for your kids, perform your job well and also be useful to others in the society. From the viewpoint of the elderly, these factors have changed and the roles have been reversed. This results in a feeling of worthlessness and low self-esteem for them.

The changes that the older adults face in terms of role reversals, dependency on their children or the loss of a spouse can be very difficult to cope. According to the perceptions of the seniors, they cease to be useful to anyone in any way and this increases their feeling of worthlessness. Their pillars of existence and the ideas of life in general begin to disappear. They go from being heroes to their kids to being dependent on their kids, a fact that they cannot accept. Simple things like driving around or even walking become an ordeal.

How To Take Great Care of Elders

Loss is always painful, be it loss of a spouse, of mobility, or health or independence. In such situations, it is no wonder that the senior citizens suffer from low self esteem. This is a precarious mental situation that may lead to depression and health problems that will prevent them from enjoying life. If there is no support system, the elderly may even turn to alcohol or drug abuse and in severe cases, suicide.

We as caregivers should try to catch the signs of low self esteem at the earliest. These may manifest in the form of sadness, or losing interest in hobbies, not taking care of oneself, not socializing or having suicidal thoughts, etc. Other symptoms may be narration of pleasant memories repetitively or trying to do things which they cannot cope with.

There are many ways to help the elderly to regain their self esteem. The first is to offer emotional support. Ensure that they are given adequate medical attention for their ailments. Another good therapy would be to allow them to spend their time in the company of their grandchildren. Encourage them to meet their friends and to talk of the old times. As a caregiver, you can be compassionate and patient while dealing with their fears and anxieties.

How To Take Great Care of Elders

Easing Into Care Giving

There is a belief that if your parents do not pass away at a young age, you will be fortunate to see them age and get the opportunity to provide them help in their old age. Very soon, as their needs and dependency increases, the occasional help may gradually change to a full fledged role of a caregiver. In some instances, the role of a caregiver comes on suddenly. This happens with the death of one parent and the widowed parent requires help and moral support to cope with the loss. For couples who have been married for decades, the sudden loss of a partner and companion is devastating and is akin to the loss of a limb. This is when your role as a caregiver is brought upon you very suddenly, and you have to look after the elderly parent's many needs.

It is always easier to move into the role of caregiver gradually, so that all the concerned persons involved, have the time to get used to the idea. Wherever possible, it is advisable to make changes in the living environment of your aged parents, so that they feel safe and comfortable in their living quarters. This may help to delay the time when they become totally dependent on you. Some things that may go a long way to help in this direction are detailed below:

- **Create the living quarters on one level.** Stairways are a danger to the elderly and it is easier on them to have everything handy at the lower level. You can adapt the plans to include the living room, bedroom, kitchen, pantry and laundry room at the ground level.
- **Reduce the daily chores to the minimum possible**, so that the elders are not tied up with this activity. Make arrangements for home delivery of groceries and food items. Arrange for a daily cleaning service for house cleaning, and someone to come and handle minor repairs and odd jobs around the house. This will take off the pressures of daily running of the household.
- **A weekly visit by a medical professional** can also be arranged, to monitor their health, keep an eye on their prescriptions and assist with any other medical requirement.
- **It is a good idea to reorganize the kitchen arrangements**, so that they are easily accessible to the elderly. For example, the shelves can be placed at eye level to store items of daily use. Appliances like the microwave and toaster should be placed in an easily accessible location.
- **Keeping their physical conditions in mind, make the house easy to use** for your parents. You can install walking and grab bars along the hall or passageways and in the

bathrooms where they may require additional support. Take care to have sufficient lighting in all the areas, so that there is good visibility.

- **There can be an arrangement of emergency pull ropes** in all rooms so that they can just pull on them to call for help in case of an emergency. These types of mechanisms are used in assisted care units, which may prove quite convenient for your aged parents to call for help in case the need arises.

By making some planned arrangements, one can make the living areas convenient, safe and comfortable for the elderly parents. This may allow them to retain their independence and help to postpone their move to a retirement home or a nursing home and also allow you to gradually ease into the role of a caregiver.

Outings For The Elderly – A Walk In The Park?

Every one needs to be outdoors and this is a crucial need for the elders too. It becomes more vital for the elders who are confined to their rooms due to lack of mobility, or any other disability. The only environment they see for days on end is within the four walls of the room and this can be frustrating enough to drive them crazy. Taking them out once in a while will be good for their mental health and keep up their spirits. With proper planning, such trips or outings can be fun and a welcome change from their mundane lives. In case a person is recovering from an illness, there is no better therapy than a breath of fresh air!

An outdoor trip for the elderly entails a lot of detailed planning before the actual outing. These cannot be undertaken spontaneously, as there are many factors to be considered. You need to first go over the activity for its suitability to the elders' condition of physical health. For instance, a person confined to a wheelchair cannot go swimming. Instead, you can arrange to take them out to the park nearby and spend some time outdoors with nature.

Day trips, shopping or talking walks in the nearby park are good outdoor activities for the elders in your care. These activities will give the elders a sense of freedom and contentment. It will ease the boredom and monotony of the routine life they lead. However, you as the caregiver should first make sure that the place you plan to take the elder in your care can accommodate them. Is there a wheelchair access at the mall you wish to go to? Can you park at a convenient place? How accessible are the restrooms? Many such questions and more need to be answered before arranging anything.

Before you leave the house, be sure to prepare for any eventuality. Carry all the medications that may be required. Ensure that there are some eatables and water with you. The seniors in your care must be wearing the appropriate clothes for the outing. There are many such checklists you must verify before you venture out of the house with the elder in your care.

An outing for the elderly in your care may not exactly be a cakewalk for you! You have to be constantly on the lookout to avoid potential mishaps or accidents. However, it is worth the effort for the pleasure it gives the old person. There is no greater feeling than seeing the person you care for smile, when they have little left in life to smile about.

Outings can make a good change for the elders in your care and you should try to incorporate them into your routine as much as possible. They promote good spirits in the elderly and remove any feelings of boredom they encounter leading to a more relaxed and healthy lifestyle.

Giving Thanks For Being A Caregiver

The role of a caregiver can be very stressful and coping with the emotional drain is a difficult challenge. There is the additional emotion of anger to cope with when the things do not go well or the feelings of resentment towards other siblings for not sharing the responsibility or even towards the parent as being the cause for all the emotional drain on you. Balancing your work, home and private life along with fulfilling the role of a caregiver can be a juggling act that few can manage well. Just as you may find the balance, the needs of your elderly parent change and you are drawn back into another stressful situation.

In order to cope with the stressful situations you may have to manage your time better to find some time for you and your family. These are not easy situations and one needs great self control and maturity to manage the stress involved. However, there is one emotion that can be said to compensate for the emotional drain that a caregiver experiences and that is thankfulness. You may be in the middle of a demanding situation and thankfulness is not usually an emotion in such times. Yet if you can be thankful for the opportunity to be the primary care giver to your parent, this positive emotion works wonders for your spirit. It helps to offset the negative emotions of anger and resentment. There are a number of things that one can be thankful for:

- You have the opportunity to repay your parents to a small extent for the sacrifices they made. All the effort, time and money that they invested in you to raise you as a good human being, is a debt that can never be repaid. But you have the occasion to return some of it in the form of caring for them in their old age. A small way to say 'Thank you for being there for me, now I am there for you.'
- If you were not staying close to your parents at the time of their need, you would have been anxious and worried about their well being. Since you are with them, you have first hand knowledge of their health conditions and anticipate any other needs that may arise.
- With the elderly, there is something always coming up causing a setback to their spirits. They need someone to give them reassurance and say that everything is all right. You have that occasion and they depend on you for moral support.
- You, as the caregiver are very important to your aged parents. They need you. You have the good fortune to be at their side during their times of crisis.

- Celebrate the times spent with each other, and enjoy the joy and laughter that you are able to share with your parent. These are the pleasant memories that will remain with you forever.

Being with a loved one through tough times and offering support, brings a sense of satisfaction to the caregiver. The bond of love between you and your parent will deepen and stay with you for the rest of your life. You may be able to look back at these pleasant memories and be thankful for the opportunity to make the final months of their life peaceful and happy.

Avoiding Guilt Pangs In The Elderly

The life of a caregiver would be very easy if he had only to do the chores and paperwork for the elderly parents. This would not be an issue if the caregiver's role was limited to this aspect. The job of taking care of the elderly is stressful to say the least. It brings about an emotional drain on the caregiver as well as the aged parent. It is assumed by both the sides that the care giving relationship is based on offering a large favor. Under the circumstances, guilt plays an important role in every element of care giving.

The senior citizen feels guilty for asking you to help out with their daily needs. In most cases, the care giver volunteered help, even though they did not ask for it. You as the caregiver, watching the situation may have intervened once you saw your parents need help in getting their life back on track. The elderly parents therefore, feel that you are spending vast amounts of your time tending to them instead of spending it with your family, or going to work. They feel guilty for imposing on your time.

The changes that the older adults face in terms of role reversals, dependency on their children or the loss of a spouse can be very difficult to cope. They feel guilty that they have ceased to be useful to anyone in any way and this increases their feeling of worthlessness. Their pillars of existence and the ideas of life in general begin to disappear. Simple things like driving around or even walking become an ordeal. They then begin to feel that had they not grown old, this would not have happened, a manifestation of guilt.

Guilt pangs are an issue with the care giver too. The constant thought of not doing enough, that certain things could have been done better is always creating these feelings of guilt. To worsen the situation the elders themselves may inflict guilt on you by complaining about their lives and not being satisfied or getting angry.

Guilt does not help improve the relationship nor does it improve the quality of life. So what does one do about this guilt running high in everyone's emotions? To stop feeling guilty is a positive step for every body. The best option would be to sit down and talk about it. Convince your parent that they need not feel guilty for taking your help, and it is not their fault that they are getting old. They too had their share of sacrifices to make when you were a child needing support.

By confronting the issue of guilt, you can avoid it affecting your relationship with the elderly parent. You should learn to avoid the guilty feelings and thus pave the way to a healthy care giver and elder relationship. Feeling guilty about things helps no one and hence these feelings are best avoided.

Safeguarding The Health Of The Elderly

We are living in a fast and materialistic world. People are concerned with materialistic pleasures and very often get their priorities wrong. They neglect their health and their relationships with their family, a consequence of leading a fast pace life. However, there are some responsibilities in life that an individual cannot neglect, and that is to care for the elders in your family. This is a special role of a caregiver that you have to undertake, to look after your elderly parents or a relative. It is a very rewarding experience, one that will remain with you in the future in the form of pleasant memories. Caring for the elderly is not an easy task and it can bring a significant amount of stress and worry upon the caregiver. The hard work is compounded if the person is infirm or disabled.

We often take our own health for granted and neglect to take care of ourselves. However, if we have the responsibility to look after our elderly parents, we have to consider many factors, and this includes their health. Here are a few tips that can help to safeguard the health of the elders in your care.

- **Diet:** Maintaining a healthy and suitable diet in respect of the elderly is of utmost importance. The older people are prone to illness more often than others and a healthy, nutritionally complete diet can keep illness at bay. Avoid large amounts of fat and salt in the diet as this slows down any recoveries from illness. Too much salt makes the circulatory system sluggish and fats can clog arteries. Instead, the diet should contain plenty of fresh fruit and vegetables to provide the necessary vitamins and minerals for the regeneration of tissues. Ensure that they get a sufficient quantity of fiber in their diet to promote bowel movement.

- **Mental Health**: The state of the mental health of the elderly individuals is a great concern for the caregiver. One has to make sure that they are comfortable in their surroundings. Setting a routine will help them relax and also give them a sense of being a part of the family life. The elderly are trying to cope with the changes happening in their lives; this may cause some depression or anxiety that should be taken care of with a little understanding and compassion.

- **Physical Health**: As a caregiver, you must ensure that the elderly in your care get regular health check ups. Any changes should be brought to the notice of the doctor immediately. This will help to diagnose problems quickly and the routine of the health checks will help the individual to relax and thus improve the general health.

- **Exercise**: It may not be possible for all elderly individuals to exercise as this depends on their physical conditions. However, 15 to 20 minutes of gentle exercise can work wonders for their general well being. Walking around the supermarket or walking the dog or gardening can be an exercise for the elders. The elderly in your care can be taken outdoors as often as possible as this can help to break the monotony of being confined to the house. Any outdoor activity will help to stretch the joints to reduce stiffness or immobility and raise their spirits, thus improving their overall health.

Protecting The Elders From Scams And Rip-Offs

Very often, the role of a caregiver is a blend of a doctor, maid, advisor and even an amateur detective. Elderly people are gullible and get regularly fleeced by smooth talking sales persons. The elderly are fiercely protective of their finances and how they use them. However, often they make wrong decisions about where to spend their money. Therefore, you as a caregiver have to look after this aspect and see that their limited resources will tide them over as long as possible.

Many senior citizens have become the victims of scams and smooth talking sales persons who sell them a hope and a dream in exchange for their money. These sales persons are constantly calling or emailing old people in the hope of getting a fast buck. If the elders become victims of a scam, it is something they try to hide from their caregivers. You as a caregiver may never know if they have been ripped off, and they will never tell you about it. Hence, you have to assume the role of an amateur detective to find out about such episodes and take steps to rectify the situation as much as possible. There may be some things you can observe to find out if your parents are victims of scams:

- Watch out for your parents' mail. If they receive large amounts of junk mail with get rich quick schemes, or phony contests, etc., it is possible that they may have become a victim of some scam.
- Spend some time at your parent's home and answer the phone there. If there are a large number of calls from charities or scam offers, then their names have got passed around to other such scam artists.
- If you see a lot of junk items lying around your parents' house, then you can be sure that they have been ripped off.
- Begin paying attention to their budget. There may be some problem with the bank account, or too many checks to con artists. Check out the credit card statement as well.
- Check out the 'sent folder' in the email account to verify any response to scam email schemes.

Your elderly parents are very often defensive of their financial activities and will resent your interference in their affairs. It takes some amount of gentle coaxing and convincing to let you see the documents. Getting involved in bogus contests or get rich quick schemes is addictive and your elderly parents are no exception to this. In spite of losing thousands of dollars to such scams, they will still get cheated by the next crook who manages to convince them, because they are addicted to it. You need to be gentle and understanding to approach the problem and find a solution.

As a caregiver, you must convince your elderly parents to let you handle their finances. You can start by handling their taxes and once they are comfortable with the idea, you can offer to take over the bill payment and manage the checkbook. Later, you can begin gently questioning the expenditure that looks suspicious to you. Do not try to get back any lost money, however, be vigilant enough to prevent any unfamiliar person from getting access to the money. Cancel all the direct debits that are not easily identifiable. Start getting a control over the phone calls, junk mail and emails. In other words, you have to play the role of a guard dog to protect your parents from scam artists and conmen out to fleece them of their money.

Making A Difference-Involving The Elderly In Social Service

The relationship between the elderly and the caregiver is a unique one. All the decisions made, revolve around the senior citizen and his needs or it is something that is worked out together to solve his problems. The world of the elderly is centered on their own physical and emotional needs.

Centering all the focus on themselves can make the senior citizen overwhelmed by compulsive habits and they begin to think that everything must begin and end with themselves. They are then not interested in being with other people and seldom go beyond thinking about themselves. This is a very unhealthy trend and can be detrimental to the mental health of the elderly.

One way of taking care of this issue is to suggest that the elder join with you to go out and do something that may be of value to others. By providing the elderly in your care an opportunity to make a difference to someone, you are encouraging them to regain their self esteem. Going out of the confines of the house into the fresh air can be a good break from their self-centered existence.

There will be much resistance to this idea of service to others by the elders initially, because they will not see any gain in it for themselves. However, you need to be very insistent and explain to them that there is life beyond themselves and the service to others will do them good, eventually.

As a caregiver, you have to plan for something simple to do, keeping in mind the physical condition of the elderly. If your mom or dad is disabled, there may be some simpler things for them to do too. Some of these are listed below:

- Take your elderly parent for a walk in the park and pick up the trash on a slow walk. This is a cleanliness drive meant to serve the society in general.
- You could take your parent to the nearby retirement home to meet someone there who would enjoy some visitors.
- Help to stuff envelopes or make telephone calls for the church or some charitable institute. This is ideal for the elderly who are confined to a wheelchair.

- You can read to the disadvantaged kids at your local library. This is again ideal for wheelchair bound elderly persons.
- You can even take a young child to the zoo or to watch the ball game, occasionally.

There are volunteer coordination agencies in most of the cities. These provide volunteering opportunities suited to the capabilities of the senior citizen. You can make use of these agencies to work out something for your elderly parent. Once the elders are out, you may be surprised at their enthusiasm for such volunteer activities.

Making a difference to others gives a great feeling of satisfaction and contentment to everyone, and more so to the elderly, because you are doing things together. This may be helpful in regaining their lost self esteem and alleviate feelings of depression or boredom. It is a good therapy for the elderly and may help to turn around their life and induce them to take a positive approach towards life.

Respecting The Rights Of Senior Citizens

There is no formal 'Senior Citizens Bill of Rights', but as individuals, senior citizens are entitled to their rights. However, the senior citizens have little energy left in them in their old age to fight for their rights and therefore, it is the duty of the children to see that their elderly parents are getting what they are rightfully entitled to.

Every right must be claimed to be deemed as a right. There are laws in existence for the running of nursing homes for the elderly and retirement communities. Even if your elderly mom or dad is in an assisted care facility, there are certain laws that are fundamental and expected to be followed by these care facilities too. It is your duty as a caregiver to see that they are following the laws and living up to the expectations.

There are some factors that you must verify before selecting a facility for your elderly parents:

- Ensure that the facility will provide the basic cleanliness and safety. Check out the evacuation plans in place, in case of an emergency situation. Verify whether the evacuation plan is a workable one, considering the fact that the facility may be full of elderly and invalids who may be slow in moving out of the building in case of a fire. Find out if there is emergency power available to operate the automatic doors and elevators so that everyone can get out safely.
- If food is provided by the facility, ensure that meals will be provided three times a day. The meals should be healthy and the food should be delivered to the room if your parent is disabled or injured. There should be some variety in the diet and since there is a separate charge for the food, it is not wrong to expect some quality and variety in the food.
- If your parent has moved to an assisted care facility, they have every right to live as they wish in that apartment, since they have paid for it. However, they have to observe certain restrictions because they are living in a community setting. They should be able to live without any interference from the staff of the facility and have the freedom to select the décor of the apartment or have family and friends to visit.
- Another fundamental right of a senior citizen is to be treated with compassion, respect and dignity. Although this is not a tangible right, how the staff at the facility treats the elderly is an important aspect in the selection of a facility for your parents. The staff of the facility must be

respectful and pleasant in their dealings with your parents. If your parent complains of any emotional or verbal abuse, you must investigate and hold the facility accountable for it.

As a primary caregiver, responsible for the well being of your elderly parents, you have the right to remind the assisted care facility of their responsibilities. Ensure that your parents are getting the service and care that they paid for and that they are comfortable in their living quarters and enjoying their stay there.

Taking Care Of Yourself As Well As The Elderly: Vacation And Respite

Caring for the elderly family member is an enormous responsibility that few people are willing to accept. The role of a caregiver is one of sacrifice in terms of their own health, family and work. When a person accepts the role of the primary caregiver to the ageing parents, he or she has no idea how long the commitment will last. It could be weeks, months or years and in that time, you as the caregiver will be mentally worn out within just a few weeks of beginning your role as the primary caregiver.

The task of the caregiver is all consuming and it will take over the control of your life very quickly, this is unavoidable. You may find it difficult to cope with the daily stress and will want to take a break very often. Either you can go away for a few days or take a break at your own home. Just like a fulltime job, this also needs recharging of your batteries.

Before thinking of respite for yourself, you have to make arrangements for the elderly in your care. Some options are available for such an eventuality. The first alternative is respite placements in a retirement home. Many retirement homes have rooms for only respite cases, so that the family members can take some rest. Before reserving a place, you can verify the home in question, by visiting the place. All the local authority offices will have details regarding such places or you can read up on the Internet.

You can opt for the home help or home care services, for the time of your absence. Home help pays visits to the elderly 3 times a day for about an hour, for washing .dressing and feeding the elderly. They do not remain with the elders throughout the day. Home care provides assistance for a longer time, but the attendant does not stay with the elderly round the clock. This may not be a good option for elders requiring constant care.

Another option is to get a family member to help out with the eldercare for the few days you will be away. This might prove to be the best choice because your mind is at ease with a familiar person looking after your elderly parent. The relatives are easily reachable at a moment's notice, to ensure proper communication. However, there must be a volunteer for this job.

Depending on your financial status, you can combine two or more options, although money is not a concern where an elders well being is involved. You must take a break as often as possible for your own health and mental peace. As a primary caregiver, you owe it to yourself and your family to take a break from the task of eldercare.

The Best Activities To Stimulate Mentally Ill Seniors

The role of a caregiver can be very stressful and coping with the emotional drain is a difficult challenge. At times, it is a challenge even to look after the best interests of the elderly in your care, especially if the person is mentally ill. A mentally ill senior will require additional care and efforts on the part of the caregiver. However, keeping a mentally ill senior occupied with some activity will take the load off your mind to a small extent.

It is essential that the mentally ill seniors keep their minds occupied with simple activities. Arranging for simple, fun activities suitable to their capabilities will provide a welcome break from the daily routine for both of you. A specific amount of time can be set aside for mentally stimulating activities during the week. For the senior this is something they begin to look forward to as it means a break in the routine. They are responding to the stimulus of the activity as a light at the end of a dark tunnel.

Elderly persons suffering from Alzheimer's disease, Dementia or Parkinson's disease must exercise their minds as much as possible. The caregiver has the task of finding the right ways to do this, but it is a difficult goal to achieve unless he has some help or advice in the matter. Therefore, the caregiver has to rely on medical advice or research that may help in achieving this goal.

Medical research shows that some forms of stimuli are better than others because of the way the mind responds to them. For instance, bright colors used in any activity get a better response and playing with brightly colored balls has worked wonders with mentally ill elders. They are able to concentrate better with bright colors around them.

However, these are just fun activities and do not serve a purpose beyond raising their spirits. Brightly colored games and puzzles can help them to sharpen their minds a little. For example, large piece jigsaw puzzles can be used to stimulate the thought processes in the elderly person's mind. They can be asked to place the pieces to complete the puzzle, with some help from the caregiver.

Outdoor activities involving animals can be suited to the mentally disabled elders. Walking a dog can be very therapeutic, bringing a sense of responsibility that was absent earlier. The task of looking after another living creature can help to lift their spirits and brighten up their life to some extent. Dogs are very loving animals and ideally suited for this purpose, because they provide an affectionate and warm response to the fuss and attention they receive. Activities such as these should be undertaken under close supervision to ensure the safety of all concerned.

As a caregiver, you must ensure that the elderly in your care remains in the best of health as much as is possible. The activities mentioned earlier can be very stimulating and beneficial to mentally ill elders and since these are done together, it is beneficial to the caregiver, too. One you start these activities and meet with success be sure to introduce some more activities to keep the elderly occupied. It helps you do your job that much better!

5 Ways To Maintain Your Health While Caring For The Elderly

Caring for the elders is a rewarding job, be it a paid employment in a nursing home or looking after an elderly relative. However, this is a mentally stressful role that may leave you exhausted to the point of desolation. Care giving requires patience and compassion and not all are able to perform this function easily. The job of care giving is easier if it is your own relative; however, it is difficult to develop the required qualities if you are taking up a paid job. Irrespective of whom you are caring for, you need to protect your own mental health in order to do your job efficiently. You can do a number of things to keep up your own perspective and mental health. A few tips are given below:

- **Take regular breaks**

Spending some time away from the elderly person you are looking after will give you the chance to relax and be away from the pressure of the job. This could be a five minute break from the work or one day off to do something you like. This will give both of you the space required to collect your thoughts and refresh yourselves. This helps to keep sight of your perspective and help to perform your role better.

- **Participate in activities that both enjoy**

Activities that both enjoy promote bonding and the common interests you share helps to build a strong base for your coexistence. If you are taking care of a stranger, you need to get to know them better. A family member is more familiar with you, so you can spend a relaxing time, together.

- **Make arrangements to suit you both**

The elderly like their independence and therefore, most of them will not expect you to be present with them throughout the day. There may be others who want you at their beck and call. You can agree on the times you will drop by to look upon them and how you will be spending the time together. This however, is not applicable to caregivers at the retirement or nursing home.

- **Establish a routine**

Setting up a routine will help the elderly to know what to expect from you and be comfortable with you. A change in the routine may upset the elderly and incite negative feelings. Most aged people do not like change and a set routine is reassuring for them. This will help you perform your role of caregiver smoothly, and may also prevent any complications that may arise in future.

- **Seek professional help**

Taking care of an elderly person is stressful to say the least. If you find that this role is leading to depression, then you must speak to a professional counselor who can provide you some help in resolving the problem. Unburdening yourself with a counselor can be a good therapy for depression, and it will help you to continue your role of caregiver.

The tips mentioned above may or may not prove beneficial to you, because it all depends on your individual circumstances. Therefore, the caregiver should study the situation and find out what works best for both.

The Caregiver's Enemy No.1

The role of a caregiver for your aged parents can be compared to fighting a battle of sorts. This becomes even more obvious in case you are caring for a terminally ill patient. You are fighting a losing battle and it will end with the passing away of your loved one. However, you are dedicated to their well being, health and happiness as much as is humanly possible so that you can make their last days as comfortable and peaceful as you can.

Your fight in this battle would be with the struggles to keep up with the medication schedules, the prescriptions and the frequency of the dosage. Another enemy you may have to face is the financial concerns. With the costs of rent, food and medical care skyrocketing, you have the constant worry of managing the funds to keep the bills paid. These are daily battles with the enemies.

The greatest enemy however, is not any of those mentioned earlier. It is not the economy or the nursing home of your mom or dad, or even any concern with your elderly parents. The biggest enemy the caregiver has to fight against is resentment. Resentment is an emotion that will hurt you as an individual and will not work well for the elderly in your care.

Resentment begins to build up in your mind even before you know what is happening. You begin to brood about little things and this hampers your ability and willingness to do the best you can for your elderly parents. Losing you as the primary caregiver is the worst situation that can happen to your ageing parents because they are totally dependent on you.

Resentment can take many forms. Some resentment may be towards the system in general. The social security and Medicare systems are changing constantly and becoming more and more complex. There may be some resentment towards the facility where your parents are residing when you feel they do not provide the necessary care to your elderly parents.

The worst kind of resentment is the one against siblings or even against the ageing parent. This is a serious problem, one that becomes so deep-rooted that it changes your perception towards your loved ones and hinders your ability to care for them. It is very easy to be overcome by the resentment towards the siblings because you may feel that the role of primary caregiver has been loaded upon you just because the others were not nearby to take the responsibility. Most often, the elderly parent appears to be demanding and ungrateful, which is the reason for your resentment towards them.

In order to overcome resentment, you have to focus your mind on the reason you are fulfilling your responsibility as a primary caregiver. You have undertaken the responsibility not for your parents or your sibling's sake, but because it is the right thing to do. You are performing your duty because your parents have taken great pains and made sacrifices to bring you up and look after you. In a way, you are trying to repay a debt which can never be repaid, in your own small way. As long as you focus on the real purpose of the mission, you can keep resentment at bay.

The Caregiver's Emotions

A caregiver's role involves many emotions and striking a balance between these emotions is a challenge for the caregiver. However, if you separate the emotions from the tasks involved in care giving, much of the things like doing grocery shopping, or the laundry, paying the bills or handling the paperwork are pretty routine. Looking after your aging parents' household chores is not caring. It is the emotional support you can provide to them in their twilight years that makes the difference.

If you are helping your elderly parent through the trial of coping with a terminal illness, they will need all the emotional support you can provide them. Although they may put up a brave front, they may be experiencing emotional turmoil due to the realization of the approaching end of their lives. As a caregiver your personal emotions at dealing with this reality, is grief. You have to try to cope with the grief together, as best as you can. At the funeral of an elderly person who has passed away due to a terminal illness, you often find that the primary caregiver is not grieving as much as the others. This is because he or she has been trying to cope with the idea for some time and has usually got used to it by then.

The two emotions associated with eldercare are compassion and pity. Your emotions as a care giver in the final months of the terminally ill elder have a direct effect on how you carry out the task of care giving. The emotion of pity involves feeling sorry for your parent's suffering whereas the emotion of compassion will make you understand the need of your parent, apart from feeling the pain, and try to help in any manner possible.

As a care giver, you have to manage your emotions and influence your reaction to the elderly parent's illness. A compassionate caregiver is most successful in his endeavor to make the elder's life comfortable. There are three important factors to keep in mind to help manage your emotions and control your reactions to the difficult times that lie ahead, and these are:

- Focus your energies and attention on the person you are caring for and not on yourself. Focusing on them builds a bond between the two of you whereas focusing on yourself will breed resentment and self pity.

How To Take Great Care of Elders

- Do not dwell on the problem, but instead try to find a solution to it. Focus on the solution to a problem and not on its effects. A good doctor will cure the disease, not the symptoms.
- Focus on the joyful moments and not on the grief and sadness. Take one day at a time and try to find moments of joy when your parents can share a good laugh with you or enjoy a meal or a good film. Being together and sharing the joys and also the pain is the core of the caregiver's role.

Keeping these three facts in mind will help to keep your emotions under control. It will also help you to function out of compassion and not pity. This will help you to keep your perspective ease the pain and grief to some extent.

Moving Your Elderly Parents Into Your Home – A Boon Or Bane?

If you as a caregiver are entrusted with the task of caring for your only surviving elderly parent, you may have to make a decision whether to move dad or mom into your home. This is a tough decision to make as you have to consider many factors. The idea projects more negative aspects than positive ones. Since you wished to live separately, you had moved out of your parents' home. To go back to living with a parent is not usually a welcome idea.

The feasibility of the idea depends on your living conditions as well. If you are single, separated or divorced, there may be space to accommodate your parent. You could combine the two homes into one and save considerable sums of money on expenses. You could also share the rent and may be even enjoy the company of your parent.

However, if you are married and have children, then there is a severe space crunch. The grandchildren will be very enthusiastic about the idea as they would like the grandparents to be with them. The adults will feel the strain of an additional member in the household.

There are more benefits about the idea of letting your mom or dad move in with you. It will save you the numerous trips to their residence; you can provide immediate attention in case of any medical problem. Food preparation can include that of the parent too and they can just become a part of the family by blending in.

However, the question of accommodating a surviving parent will provoke a different reaction from the experts in eldercare. They would advise against accommodating them in your house, and to avoid it as much as possible. Parents have the habit of interfering with child discipline or marital spats. They will also be nosey about teenagers' issues. This will create discord among all the members of the family.

Teenagers do not like to answer questions and more so with inquisitive grandparents around. You have some conflict resolutions systems in place that work on each other's understanding. The systems work because each one can understand the signs. An elderly parent would be out of place in such as situation.

The main reason for not having your mom or dad live with you is because you as a primary caregiver need some respite and should be able to get away from the elderly at least for a short while. The role of primary caregiver is stressful, so it is good for you to go home and forget the worries for a while. You need to preserve the sanctuary, to maintain your sanity and health. This will prove to be beneficial to the caregiver as well as the receiver and all the others in the family too. After all, each one needs the space to unwind and refresh, and maybe your mom or dad needs it too!

This Product Is Brought To You By

www.ingramcontent.com/pod-product-compliance
Lightning Source LLC
LaVergne TN
LVHW021054100526
838202LV00083B/5883